Kidfiddle

46 Easy Folk Songs for Fiddle with Chordal Accompaniment

By Jerry Silverman

A Note From Jerry Silverman

Each of the fiddle and folk tunes in this collection has been presented in more than one key. This will permit teachers to introduce the all-important concept of tonality early in their students' musical development. It will also help the students' musical accuracy in terms of finding half-step differences as the keys change.

All the tunes have been harmonized with chord symbols. If teacher, parent, or friend can accompany these tunes on the guitar, autoharp, piano, or other chord-playing instrument, the benefit to the student will be readily apparent.

Almost all the tunes are in the first position

2 3 4 5 6 7 8 9 0

D1088487

Contents

Cripple Creek

She'll Be Comin' 'Round The Mountain

Key of D

Key of G

Old Joe Clark

Key of A
(Mixolydian Mode — Two Sharps)

Key of D
(Mixolydian Mode — One Sharp)

Yankee Doodle

Key of D

Key of G

Red River Valley

Key of C

Key of D

Filimiooriay

Key of E minor

Key of A minor

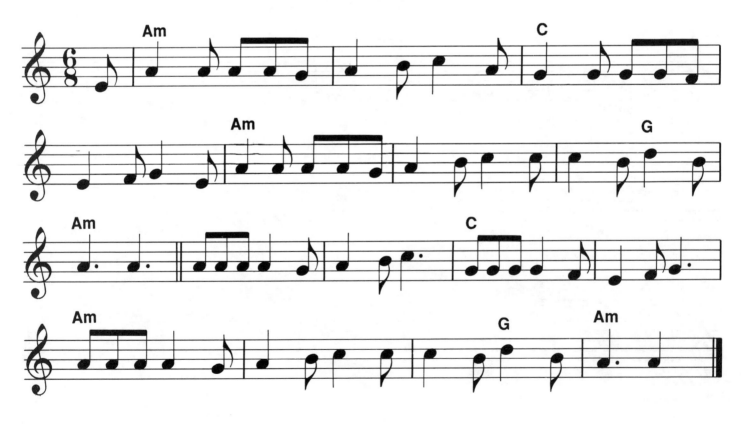

Rig A Jig Jig

Key of A

Key of C

Camptown Races

Key of A

Key of D

Liza Jane

Key of G

Key of C

Skip To My Lou

Key of C

Key of G

Key of D

Flop - Eared Mule

Key of D

Key of G

Key of C

13

Cindy

Key of A

Key of C

Old Dan Tucker

Key of A

Key of E

Old Rosin, The Beau

Key of F

Key of G

On Top Of Old Smoky

Key of G

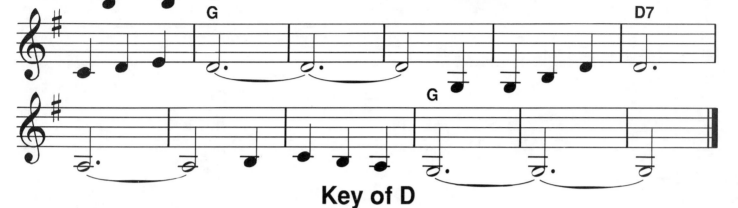

Key of D

Key of A

Crossing Over To Ireland

Key of A minor

Key of E minor

Key of B minor

Home On The Range

Key of G

Key of C

Crawdad

Key of A

Key of C

Black-Eyed Susie

Bowling Green

Bury Me Beneath The Willow

Key of A

Key of C

Key of G

Cumberland Gap

Darling Cory

Key of D
(Mixolydian Mode — One Sharp)

Key of G
(Mixolydian Mode — No Sharps)

Key of E
(Mixolydian Mode — Three Sharps)

Fly Around My Blue - Eyed Gal

Key of E

Key of G

Key of G
(8ve higher)

Mama Don't 'Low

Key of E

Key of G

More Pretty Girls Than One

Ground Hog

Key of E minor

Key of A minor

Key of D minor

My Home's Across The Smoky Mountains

Key of D

Key of A

Sail Away, Ladies

Key of A

Key of C

Sally Ann

Key of D

Key of D
(8ve higher)

Key of G

Red Apple Juice

Key of F

Key of G

Key of A

Sally Goodin

Key of A

Key of G

Sourwood Mountain

Key of A

Key of C

Key of E

The Wabash Cannonball

Key of G

Key of C

Salty Dog

Key of D

Key of E

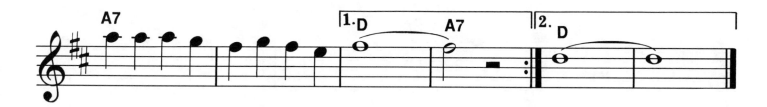

Key of A

The Wreck Of The Old 97

Key of A

Key of G

Nine Hundred Miles

Key of A minor

Key of E minor

Arkansas Traveler

Key of D

Key of G

The Gal I Left Behind Me

Oh, Them Golden Slippers

Key of C

Key of E

Captain Jinks

Key of C

Key of D

Mountain Dew

Key of A

Key of C

The Irish Washerwoman

Key of C

Key of G

Garryowen

Key of D

Key of G

Turkey In The Straw

Key of D

Key of C

Ragtime Annie

Key of G

Key of D